English Verb Tenses

at a Glance

A color---coded verb guide for ESL Students

(and teachers!)

A supplement to any ESL textboo

Randi Wissler-Mitchell

Wall-sized and fold-out charts for the classroom available at: **www.randimitchell.com**

Dedication

This book is dedicated to my intermediate ESL students who needed to learn 15 different English verb constructions, and their meanings, in a three--- week summer course. They wanted to easily understand, "at a glance," how all the tenses work together, what they mean, and why we say them when we do. Together, we developed a system to see all of the verb tenses on one page and on a timeline. The book is also dedicated to the ESL students whom I have taught in past four years and who have watched the charts evolve from magic marker drawings into wall charts and laminates made by a professional graphic artist. These students have helped me to get the errors out of the worksheets and exercises. Each year the charts and worksheets have gotten better, but the basic concept has never changed. The color---coordinated charts and exercises help the students visualize and recall the proper usage of the tenses.

I have used the following charts, posters and worksheets ever since that short summer session. I find that the color---coded system is an easy and fun method for teaching the tenses quickly.

Acknowledgments

I thank Mimi Parris for suggesting that I publish my charts. I am also thankful to Mary---Gordon Spence for her encouragement and editing. Jane Froelich did a great job of turning all my magic marker drawings and ideas into graphics. I have deep gratitude, also, to Jenny Meadows, who spent many hours on this text at My Copy Editor. Trying to get the colors correct in the text will make anyone crazy. And thanks to John Schmidt, my Academic Advisor, and to my family, Tom Hefter and J'aime Mitchell, for their ideas, support and patience in the past four years. I am especially grateful to Ms. Betty Azar, whom I consider to be a "grammar guru." I used Ms. Azar's book to get my TEFL certificate in Peru, and I always refer to her books and charts when I am tryng to understand grammar concepts for myself and explain them to my students. I was honored that she was gracious enough to take the time to read my ideas and respond to me with kind suggestions and encouragement.

Preface

I realize that the term "tense" is used loosely in this book. This is for the purpose of simplifying an already difficult subject for ESL students. Our verbs actually have tenses and aspects. Tense is more concerned with time, whereas the aspect of a verb indicates completion, duration, or repetition of an action.

The tenses of our verbs are only <u>past</u> and <u>present</u>. The primary aspects in English are the <u>simple,</u> the <u>perfect,</u> and the <u>progressive</u>. The **Simple Aspect** is sometimes called zero aspect, as it is in base form, except for third person singular. The **Perfect Aspect** describes events occurring in the past but linked to a later time, present (present perfect) or past (past perfect.) The perfect aspect is formed with *has, have,* or *had* + the *past participle.* The **Progressive Aspect** usually describes an event that takes place during a limited time period. The progressive aspect is made up of a form of *be* + the ---*ing form of the main verb.* (also known as the *continuous* form).

The two aspects of perfect and progressive may be combined to form the **Perfect Progressive.** Traditionally, the aspects are treated as part of the tense system in English, and we commonly speak of tenses such as the Simple, Progressive, Perfect, and Perfect Progressive in past, present and future.

Many people are surprised to be told that English has no future tense — and for everyday purposes I find that it isn't a particularly helpful way of describing how English verbs work. It's more useful to talk about entire verb phrases and to look at the way they give information about time and aspect. The 12 traditional tenses are actually a combination of tense and aspect. For the purpose of the book, which is a manual for ESL learners, I prefer to use the easiest system of classification for the learners. For the sake of simplicity and the purpose of this manual, I will be talking about "tenses" in the following forms:

	SIMPLE	**PROGRESSIVE**	**PERFECT**	**PERFECT PROGRESSIVE**
PAST	I walked	I was walking	I had walked	I had been walking
PRESENT	I walk	I am walking	I have walked	I have been walking
FUTURE	I will walk	I will be walking	I will have walked	I will have been walking

A color---coded chart of the commonly used English tenses is found in Appendix A5. The chart is part of the section that has perforated pages for students to tear out and use for reference. The other 2 charts are divided into the present and past tenses on one chart and the future tenses on the other.

Table of Contents

Introduction

These charts are a product of my students' frustration.

I taught an intensive three-week summer course for intermediate ESL students one summer. In a survey of what they wanted to learn, the majority of students said that they were frustrated with English verb tenses and wanted to know how and when to use them properly. I tried to find a chart online or in a book that demonstrated the timeline of all the tenses together. I could not find one, so I decided that we would design one.

I say that we designed the charts together because I used deductive reasoning with my students. I explained each tense and then we practiced it. At the end of each practice session with the verb tense, I asked the students how they thought it should be drawn on the chart. We kept a poster board of the past tenses on the wall, which the entire class could see as a reference. Then we did the same thing with the future tenses. Since that class, the posters have been refined over and over again to get them into graphic form. Now when I teach tenses, I give each student a personal copy of the charts, and we keep the large posters on the wall. The large posters have been graphically reproduced so that teachers may use them during a unit of verb tense analysis. (They now available under the same name: "Tenses at A Glance"-posters: "Present and Past Tenses at Glance" and "Future Tenses at a Glance.")

In my current classes, the students constantly use the charts until the tenses and their names became second nature. At the end of the present/ past tense unit, we switch to the future tenses chart. When we are finished with all the different tenses in past, present, and future, I put the two large posters together on the wall. The students are always amazed to see all the tenses together and how much they have learned.

I have used individual charts and the wall posters ever since that three -week course, and I find that it is an easy and fun method for teaching the tenses quickly. Last semester I had students from other classes coming to take pictures of the posters for future use. One of them asked me why I didn't publish the posters, and that lead to the writing of this book.

This book offers an overview of the most commonly used tenses in English and is meant to be a supplemental guide for ESL students. It is not a substitute for a textbook, but rather a tool to help the students see the timeline of our tenses and how they all fit together. I also give some words that signal each tense in exams and in speaking.

I cover the main tenses in past, present, and future. I also cover conditional and time clauses for the future. I realize that all the tenses in English are not covered, but the main ones are explained and available on perforated charts at the end of the book. There is also a laminated version in a pocket in the back of the book. Here students and teachers will find the tools for a basic understanding of the most commonly used verb tenses in English.

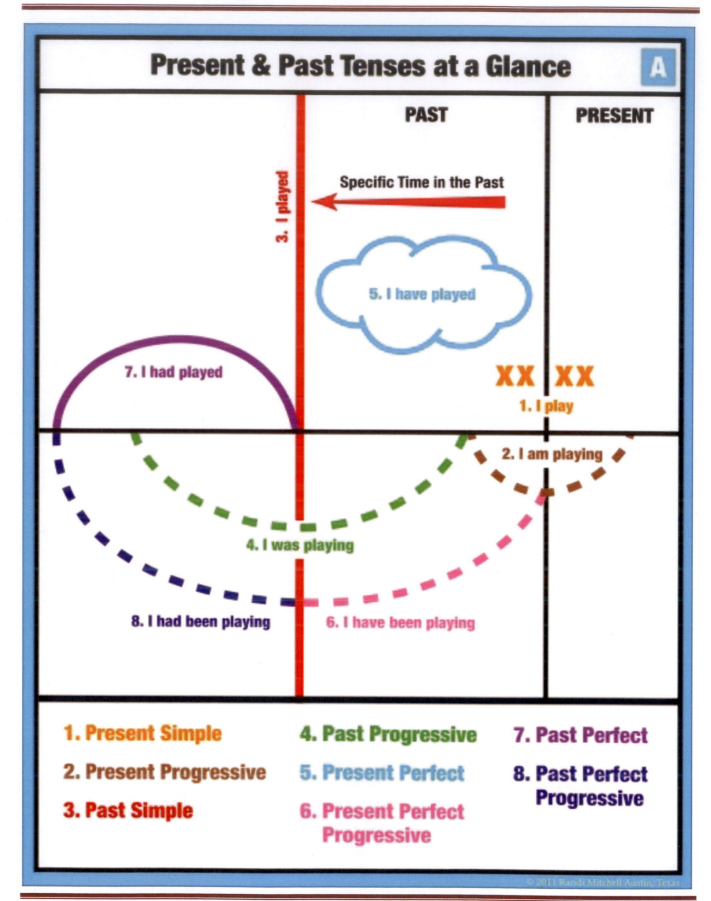

Part One: Present and Past Tenses

Explanation of Chart A: "Present and Past Tenses at a Glance"

a) The curved dotted lines mean "activity," "progression" – something that is on-going for a length of time. (These are the progressive tenses.)

b) The solid curved lines mean that an action or event is completed.

c) The solid vertical lines represent a specific time. (Black = Present / Red = Past)

1) **PRESENT SIMPLE** is represented by the orange "X X X X" that crosses the line from past to present, because present tense is used for facts, habits, and routines that can always happen or be true. (They are not just in the present.) The frequency depends on the *adverb of frequency* used with it.

2) **PRESENT PROGRESSIVE** is represented by the brown dotted line that is under the word "Present." (It is happening right now.)

3) **PAST SIMPLE** is indicated by the solid red vertical line, and it represents a specific time in the past that a certain activity or event began or ended. It also represents an event at a specific time in the past. The other past tenses revolve around this red line. The Past Perfect can be seen only BEFORE the solid red line, and Present Perfect can only be seen AFTER the solid red line. Past Progressive is intersected by this red line, which represents a specific time in the past that an action was happening, or another event in the past which interrupted the on-going action.

4) **PAST PROGRESSIVE** is shown as a green dotted line. The action started at some time in the past and was ongoing at a specific time in the past or when a different past action occurred. It is intersected by the red line which represents a specific time in the past or an event in **Past Simple.** A **Past Progressive** on-going action, which is interrupted by a **Past Simple** event, can stop or continue, depending on the situation.

5) **PRESENT PERFECT** tense is in a cloud, because it can float. It is "nebulous" and hazy. There is no specific time attached to it, except that it happened sometime in the past and is somehow relevant to the present conversation. (It cannot, however, come before another event in the past.)

6) **PRESENT PERFECT PROGRESSIVE** is shown with a pink dotted line which goes from the red **Past Simple** to the vertical black line representing present. This illustrates an activity that started at a certain time in the past and continues until the present.

7) **PAST PERFECT** is shown by the purple solid line ending at the RED line for **Past Simple.** It must be used to show the relationship between two past events: If an event happened BEFORE the **Past Simple** is used, it will be in **Past Perfect.**

8) **PAST PERFECT PROGRESSIVE** is seen as a blue dotted line that represents an activity that had been going on before a time or event in the **Past Simple** interrupted it.

What do the Tenses mean?

1) Present Simple: "I play"

- The **Present Simple** tense is represented by the orange **"XX XX"** that crosses over into the past, the present, and the future. This is because the simple present can always be true, not simply in the immediate present. In other words, if I say "I love football," I not only love it today, but I probably loved it yesterday, and I will still love it tomorrow.

- **Habits, Routines, Facts:**
  "I go to bed at 7:00." (habit)
  "I play soccer on Thursdays." (routine)
  "The sky is blue." (fact)

- Form the **Present Simple** by using the base form for all subjects except the <u>third person singular</u> (he, she, it). *The third person singular conjugates by adding "s" to any verb.
  *(See Appendix **A1** for spelling rules to add "s" to verbs.)

Note: In all of the following charts, "you" also refers to plural.

PRESENT SIMPLE STATEMENTS: Affirmative			
I	**eat**	he	**eats**
you	**eat**	she	**eats**
we	**eat**	it	**eats**
they	**eat**		

Words that signal the Present Simple:

Rarely	Seldom	Usually
Never	Generally	Always
Every day	Typically	Sometimes
Frequently	In general	Normally

(any adverbs of frequency)

"I **always study** at the library."

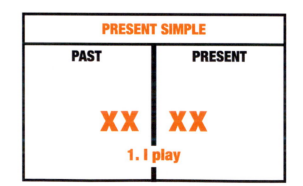

Practice: Present Simple

Use the verb that is in parentheses and change it to the Present Simple tense.

1. I always _____ (study) at home.

2. She often _____ (study) in a coffee shop.

3. He never _____ (eat) fast food.

4. They sometimes _____ (go) to the Bahamas.

5. I _____ (drive) to school most of the time.

Questions: Form questions with "Do" or "Does":

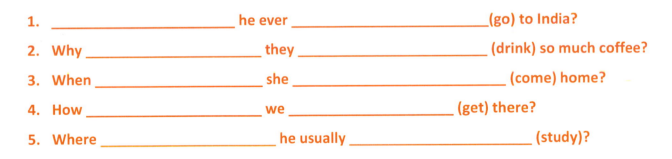

PRESENT SIMPLE QUESTIONS			
Do	I?	**Does**	he?
Do	you?	**Does**	she?
Do	we?	**Does**	it?
Do	they?		

Use the verb that is in parentheses and change it to make Present Simple questions:

1. _____ he ever _____(go) to India?

2. Why _____ they _____ (drink) so much coffee?

3. When _____ she _____ (come) home?

4. How _____ we _____ (get) there?

5. Where _____ he usually _____ (study)?

Negative: I don't, You don't, We don't, They don't

        He doesn't, She doesn't, It doesn't

Use the verb that is in parentheses and change it to make Present Simple negative:

1. She _____ (not/ go) to school on Saturdays.

2. They _____ (not/ want) any ice cream.

2) Present Progressive: "I am playing"

- The **Present Progressive** is marked by the brown dotted line which crosses the vertical black line that says "**PRESENT.**" This tense means that something is happening *right now.*

- **Present Progressive** means that an activity is in progress right now.
  "Don't bother me. I'm studying right now."

- It can mean that something is temporary or changing.
  "I'm living with my aunt until I can find an apartment."

- We form the **Present Progressive** by using a *conjugated* form of the verb "BE" with the base form of a verb and "ing." BE is conjugated with the subject.*

  *See Appendix **A2** for spelling rules of progressive forms.

  Examples: "I **am talking** on the phone right now."   "He **is writing** a letter."

  Present Progressive is formed as follows: Subject **+ be + verb + ing**

PRESENT PROGRESSIVE STATEMENTS: Affirmative			
I	**am writing**	he	**is writing**
you	**are writing**	she	**is writing**
we	**are writing**	it	**is writing**
they	**are writing**		

Some words that signal Present Progressive:

Right now	**This week**
At the moment	**This year**
Right this minute	**This semester**
Currently	**These days****

**** Signals something temporary or changing:
"She's not feeling well these days."**

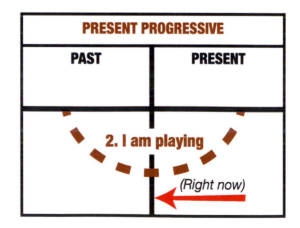

Practice: Present Progressive.

Use the verb that is in parentheses and change it to the Present Progressive tense.

1. Right now I _____ (talk) to my friend on the phone.

2. They _____ (not/play) cards at the moment.

3. Look! It_____! (rain)

4. Jasmine normally walks to school, but today she _____ (ride) her bike.

5. I usually study at home, but tonight I_____ (go) to the library.

Questions are formed with a *conjugated* form of: "BE" + subject + verb + ing?

PRESENT PROGRESSIVE QUESTIONS					
Am	I	**dreaming?**	**Is**	he	**dreaming?**
Are	you	**dreaming?**	**Is**	she	**dreaming?**
Are	we	**dreaming?**	**Is**	it	**dreaming?**
Are	they	**dreaming?**			

Use the verb in parentheses to make Present Progressive questions:

1. _____ he _____ (leave) the party now?

2. Why _____ you _____ (smoke) in the building?

3. Where _____ she _____ (go)?

4. When _____ he _____ (take) the quiz?

5. _____ they _____ (study) at the library?

Negative: 1st way: I'm not writing, You're not writing, We're not writing, They're not writing.

He's not writing, She's not writing, It's not writing

2nd way: I'm not writing, You aren't writing, We aren't writing, They aren't writing,

He isn't writing, She isn't writing, It isn't writing

Use the verb in parentheses to make Present Progressive negative:

1. They_____ (not/ take) an English class this semester.

2. She _____ (not/ study) right now.

2a) Stative Verbs - (Present Simple vs. Present Progressive)

Some verbs describe **states and conditions.** They are normally used in the **Present Simple.**

Examples:

Description: appear, be, exist, look, seem, sound

Measurement: cost, weigh

Emotion: feel, hate, love, prefer, like, need, want, care, mind, appreciate

Possession: belong, contain, have, need, own, want, depend on, consist of, get

Sense: hear, smell, taste, see, ache, burn

Perception: notice, see, understand

Knowledge: believe, forget, know, remember, think, recognize, notice, guess, hope,

mean, understand, agree, disagree, doubt, feel (think)

Exceptions: If the verb indicates an action in progress right now.

1. **The soup tastes good.**   **I am tasting the soup to see if it needs salt.**

    (outside influence-involuntary)   (action by the person-voluntary)

2. **I smell something awful.**   **I'm smelling the candles to see which one to buy.**

    (outside influence-involuntary)   (action by the person - voluntary)

3. **My kids are normally well-behaved.**   Today they **are being** awful!

    (typical behavior)   (not typical behavior)

4. **Tom has 3 cars.**   **I'm having a good time at your party.**

    (possession)   (experience)

5. **I see the school.**   **I am seeing the doctor today.**

    (sensory)   (action "going to")

6. **I think you are nice.**   **I am thinking about my vacation.**

    (belief)   (using the brain right now)

2b) Practice: Stative or Action_words

Cover the answers below and practice choosing the active or stative meaning.

Circle the form of the verb which completes the sentence correctly.

1. It **(appears / is appearing)** to be foggy outside.

2. The doctor **(believes / is believing)** that I have the flu.

3. Sara usually **(gets / is getting)** good grades on tests.

4. You **(are / are being)** really stubborn today!

5. Tommy **(has / is having)** a good time at the birthday party.

6. You **(don't seem / aren't seeming)** like yourself today.

7. What **(do you think/are you thinking)** about? You look so far away!

8. I **(don't think / am not thinking)** the school is open on Saturday.

9. Something **(smells / is smelling)** rotten.

10. Sam **(tastes / is tasting)** the whipped cream to see if it needs sugar.

11. That cake is nice. How much **(does it cost / is it costing)**?

12. **(Do you see / Are you seeing)** that red car?

ANSWERS: 1. appears 2. believes 3. gets 4. are being 5. is having 6. don't seem 7. are you thinking 8. don't think 9. smells 10. is tasting 11. does it cost 12. Do you see

3) Past Simple: "I played"

- The **Past Simple** is shown by a solid red line, because this is a <u>specific</u> time or event in the past. It can interrupt another past tense (past progressive) or signal the beginning (present perfect) or ending (past perfect) of other past actions.
- Use the **Past Simple** to express the idea that an action started and finished at a specific time in the past.
  "I played soccer yesterday.
- Form the simple past by adding **"ed"** to regular verbs,*
   or by using the **2nd form** of irregular verbs.**

  *See appendix **A3** for spelling rules of "ed" endings on regular verbs.
  See Appendix **A4 for a list of irregular verbs. (The second form is in red.)

The past form stays the same for all persons:

PAST SIMPLE STATEMENTS: Affirmative			
I	**asked**	he	**asked**
you	**asked**	she	**asked**
we	**asked**	it	**asked**
they	**asked**		

Some signal words for Past Simple:

Yesterday	Before
A month ago	After
In 2008	Last week, last year,
When	Last Time
Specific time:	"Yesterday I went to the zoo."

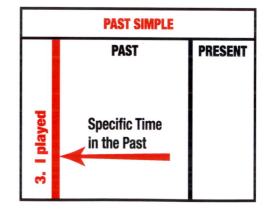

Note: Sometimes, in informal speaking, people use *already* and *yet* with past simple.

In academic writing, use *already* and *yet* with present perfect.

Practice: Past Simple

Use the verb in parentheses and change it to the **Past Simple** tense.

1. Yesterday I _____ (go) to the zoo.
2. Last week my friend _____ (come) to visit.
3. I _____ (meet) that girl two years ago.
4. The last time I _____ (speak) with her, we _____ (have) a fight.
5. I _____ (teach) English in 2008.

Questions: Form **Past Simple** questions as follows: **"Did"** + subject + **base form of the verb.**

"Did" stays the same for all persons.

PAST SIMPLE QUESTIONS			
Did I **play?**		**Did** he **play?**	
Did you **play?**		**Did** she **play?**	
Did we **play?**		**Did** it **play?**	
Did they **play?**			

Use the verb in parentheses to make **Past Simple** questions:

1. _____ she _____ (go) to the party?
2. _____ he_____ (stay) late?
3. When _____ you _____ (see) her?
4. Why _____ they _____ (ask) her to quit?
5. Where _____ we _____ (get) that cat?

Negative: I didn't play, You didn't play, We didn't play, They didn't play

He didn't play, She didn't play, It didn't play

Use the verb in parentheses and change it to make **Past Simple** negative:

1. I _____ (not/ go) to the party last night.

2. She _____ (not/ see) the movie last night.

4) Past progressive: "I was playing"

- **PAST PROGRESSIVE** is shown as a green dotted line, which means an ongoing action. It crosses the vertical red line that indicates a specific time in the past. This line can be a specific time in the past, or an event in the **Past Simple.**

- **Past Progressive** means than an action was going on at a specific time in the past. "At 2:00, I **was studying."**

- It can mean that an action was going on when something else in the **Past Simple** happened. "We **were talking** about her when **she walked** in."

- A **past progressive** on-going action which is interrupted by a **Past Simple** event can stop or continue, depending on the situation:

I was studying when you called. (Perhaps the action of studying continued.)

I was dancing when I broke my leg. (Most likely, the action of dancing stopped.)

Past progressive is formed as follows: Subject + was/ were + verb + ing

PAST PROGRESSIVE STATEMENTS: Affirmative			
I	**was playing**	he	**was playing**
you	**were playing**	she	**was playing**
we	**were playing**	it	**was playing**
they	**were playing**		

Some signal words for Past Progressive:

When + Past Simple: (When you called,)

At that time

At 2:00 (at + time in the past)

While

Meanwhile

In the meantime

Last week

Then   **At that time**

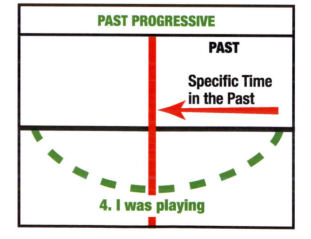

Practice: Past Progressive

Use the verb in parentheses to form the Past Progressive:

1. I _____ (study) **when they came.**

2. **I didn't hear** the doorbell, because I _____ (take) a shower.

3. While the firemen _____ (save) the people, the policeman

   _____ (talk) on the loudspeaker.

4. **I didn't hear** the teacher, because I _____ (daydream).

5. I _____ (listen) to the radio **when I heard** the news.

Questions are formed as follows: Was/ Were + subject + verb + ing?

PAST PROGRESSIVE QUESTIONS					
Was	I	**playing?**	**Was**	he	**playing?**
Were	you	**playing?**	**Was**	she	**playing?**
Were	we	**playing?**	**Was**	it	**playing?**
Were	they	**playing?**			

Use the verb in parentheses to form Past Progressive questions:

1. What _____you _____ (do) last night?

2. _____ he (talk) _____ about me **when I came** in?

3. Why _____ you (talk) _____ **when the bell rang?**

4. _____the students still _____ (stand) **when the teacher came** in?

5. What _____ you (look) _____for **when I saw** you at the mall?

Negative: I wasn't playing, You weren't playing, We weren't playing, They weren't playing

   He wasn't playing, She wasn't playing, It wasn't playing

Use the verb in parentheses to form Past Progressive negative:

1. We _____(not/listen) to the teacher **when she gave** instructions.

2. He _____ (not/ study) **when I walked** in.

5) Present Perfect: "I have played"

- The Present Perfect is shown in the turquoise cloud because it can "float." It is "nebulous" and hazy, because the time of the action is not important or specific. It can be in the far distant past or in the recent past. The cloud helps students to remember *"no specific time."*

- Unspecified time in the past (NEVER use a specific time with Present Perfect)
  You *CANNOT* say: "I have gone to the park *yesterday*."
  The action may or may not be still going on, but it is relevant to the present.
  Example: "I have been to Paris." (Paris, or traveling, is part of the conversation.)

- We can use Present Perfect for events that continue into the present. For this we use "for" and "since". Examples: I have lived here for 3 years. " " I have lived here since 2010."
  ("Since" is the only word that takes a specific time in this tense.)

- We use Present Perfect for repeated actions in the past.
  "I have seen that movie 3 times."

- Form Present Perfect with **Subject +** have **or** has **+past participle of the main verb**
  "Have" is conjugated to agree with the subject. The past participle never changes.

Examples: "She has played 3 times." "They have played 3 times."

PRESENT PERFECT STATEMENTS: Affirmative			
I	have played	he	has played
you	have played	she	has played
we	have played	it	has played
they	have played		

Signal words for Present Perfect:

Yet	Ever	Number of times
Already	Never	("I have been to
Just	Recently	Spain 3 times.")
So far	Up to now	

Since (use with specific date)

For (use with amount of time)

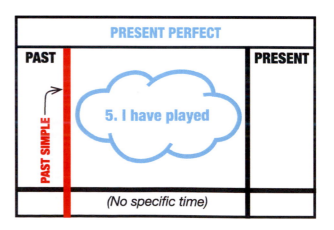

Practice: Present Perfect

Use the verb in parentheses to form the present perfect tense:

(Remember- "Have" is conjugated with the subject.)

1. I _____ (never/see) anything like it!

2. _____ (you/ever/ go) to Europe?

3. I _____ (just/ finish) my homework.

4. Are you hungry? No, I _____ (already/ eat.)

5. She _____ (live) there for two years.

Questions:

Use **Have** or **Has** with past participle. (**Have** is conjugated to go with the subject.)

Examples: **Have you done your homework? Has she done her homework?**

PRESENT PERFECT QUESTIONS			
Have I **worked?**		**Has** he **worked?**
Have you **worked?**		**Has** she **worked?**
Have we **worked?**		**Has** it **worked?**
Have they **worked?**		

Use the verb in parentheses to form Present Perfect questions:

1. Why _____ he _____ (eat) all the fruit?

2. When _____ you ever _____ (do) anything for me?

3. How often _____ they _____ (visit) you?

4. _____ you _____ (see) any good movies lately?

5. _____ he _____ (do) anything fun recently?

Negative: I haven't worked, You haven't worked, We haven't worked, They haven't worked

He hasn't worked, She hasn't worked, It hasn't worked.

Use the verb in parentheses to form **Present Perfect** negative:

1. You _____ (not/ work) since last summer.

2. He _____ (not/ be) to Paris yet.

6) Present Perfect Progressive: "I have been playing"

- **Present Perfect Progressive** is shown on the chart in a pink dotted line starting at the red line for **Past Simple** and reaching the black vertical line for present, to show that it is an activity which began at a certain time in the past and continues until present.

- We use the **Present Perfect Progressive** to show that something started at a specific time in the past and has continued up until now or just recently.

Examples: "I have been working for five minutes," "for two weeks," "since Tuesday,"

  - or "I have been studying for 2 hours now."

Form **Present Perfect Progressive** with

Subject + **have or has** + **been** +**main verb** + **ing**

PRESENT PERFECT PROGRESSIVE **STATEMENTS:** Affirmative					
I	**have been studying**		he	**has been studying**	
you	**have been studying**		she	**has been studying**	
we	**have been studying**		it	**has been studying**	
they	**have been studying**				

Signal Words for Present Perfect Progressive:

The whole week

For 4 years (amount of time)

Since 1993 (specific time)

All day "I have been working all day!"

Note: Do not use <u>number of times</u> with progressive tenses.

No!!! I have been reading this book 3 times.

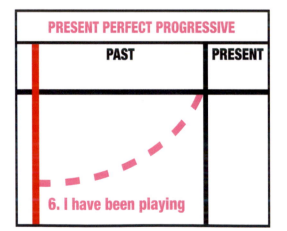

PRESENT PERFECT PROGRESSIVE

	PAST	PRESENT

6. I have been playing

Practice: Present Perfect Progressive

Use the word in parentheses to make the Present Perfect Progressive.

1. I _____ (work) on this project all day!

2. She _____ (study) for three hours now.

3. My dad _____ (travel) to Asia lately.

4. We _____ (visit) them since I was a child.

5. He _____ (go) there since he was five.

Questions: Form Questions with Have or Has + subject + been + verb + ing

(Have is conjugated with the subject.)

PRESENT PERFECT PROGRESSIVE QUESTIONS			
Have I been playing?		Has he been playing?	
Have you been playing?		Has she been playing?	
Have we been playing?		Has it been playing?	
Have they been playing?			

Use the word in parentheses to make the Present Perfect Progressive questions:

1. _____ she _____(study) a lot lately?

2. Where _____ he _____ (go) at night?

3. Why _____ they _____ (stay) home so much?

4. _____ you _____(eat) out recently?

5. _____ we _____(miss) anything important?

Negative: I haven't been playing, You haven't been playing, We haven't been playing,
They haven't been playing
He hasn't been playing, She hasn't been playing, It hasn't been playing.

Use the word in parentheses to make the Present Perfect Progressive negative:

1. You _____(not/ ask) questions like I told you to do.

2. She _____(not/ take) her vitamins lately.

7) Past Perfect: "I had played"

- The Past Perfect is represented by the purple solid line which ends at the red line for Past Simple. This means it is an event that took place before a certain time or event in the past.

- **Past Perfect takes place before another event in the past.**

- The **Past Perfect** shows the relationship of *two past events.*
  Past Perfect is "married" to the Past Simple - we don't use it unless there is another event in the the past it is related to. The event in Past Perfect is the first event. The event in Past Simple is the second event.

  "**I had already left** by the time she got there."
  (1) I left first; then (2) she got there.

Form the **Past Perfect** with: Subject + **had + past participle of main verb.**

("**Had**" does not change with the subject.)

PAST PERFECT STATEMENTS: Affirmative			
I	**had eaten**	he	**had eaten**
you	**had eaten**	she	**had eaten**
we	**had eaten**	it	**had eaten**
they	**had eaten**		

Signal words for Past Perfect:

Never

For

Before

When

Yet

By the time – "By the time I got there, she had left."

After - "After I had eaten, I took a shower."

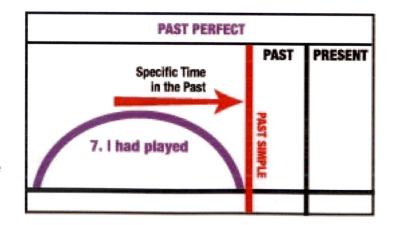

Practice: Past Perfect

Use the verb in parentheses and change it to make Past Perfect:

1. **I was late** for work, because I _____ (miss) the bus.

2. **We lived** in a house that my father _____ (build.)

3. As soon as the students _____ (finish) the tests, the **teacher graded** them.

4. I _____(guess) the ending before **I finished** the whole book.

5. After I _____ (shower), **I went** to bed.

Questions in PAST PERFECT are formed as follows: Had+ subject + past participle

PAST PERFECT QUESTIONS				
Had	I	**seen?**	**Had** he	**seen?**
Had	you	**seen?**	**Had** she	**seen?**
Had	we	**seen?**	**Had** it	**seen?**
Had	they	**seen?**		

Use the verb in parentheses and change it to make Past Perfect questions:

1. _____ you ever _____(see) mountains before **we came** to Colorado?

2. _____ he _____(know) about the party before **you told** him?

3. _____ she _____(do) her homework before **you asked** her to?

4. How often _____ they _____ (come) to visit before **you moved** back home?

5. _____ you _____(be) hired before **she left** the job?

Negative: I hadn't seen, You hadn't seen, We hadn't seen, They hadn't seen,

   He hadn't seen, She hadn't seen, It hadn't seen

Use the verb in parentheses and change it to make Past Perfect negative:

1. He _____(not/see) that movie before **last night.**

2. She _____(never/ hear) of body language before **she saw that video.**

8) Past Perfect Progressive: "I had been playing"

- The **Past Perfect Progressive** is represented by the broken blue line which ends at the red line for **Past Simple.**

  - Indicates a continuous action that was completed at some point in the past. It is stopped by a past time or an event in the **Past Simple.**
  - Use the progressive tense to stress the <u>length of time</u> or the <u>action.</u>
  - Just like the past perfect, the past perfect progressive happens first; then something else happens in the **Past Simple.**

  "I had been studying for 3 hours when I finally **fell asleep.**"

  (1st action)   (2nd action)

Form the Past Perfect Progressive with:

Subject + had + past participle of "be" + verb + ing

PAST PERFECT PROGRESSIVE STATEMENTS: Affirmative		
I **had been eating**	he	**had been eating**
you **had been eating**	she	**had been eating**
we **had been eating**	it	**had been eating**
they **had been eating**		

Signal words for Past Perfect Progressive:

Never	When
For	By the time
Before	After
By then	By 2:00

(Some event, or time, <u>**in the past,**</u> ended the progression)

Examples: "**By 2:00** I had been working on this project for 3 hours."

"**By the time she got** there, I had been working for 3 hours."

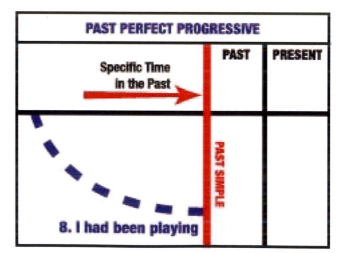

Practice: Past Perfect Progressive

Use the verb in parentheses to form the Past Perfect Progressive:

1. She **spilled** paint on the canvas she _____ (paint).

2. We **admired** the picture she _____ (draw).

3. My cat **spilled** milk on the floor I _____ (clean).

4. I _____ (work) on that paper for 3 hours before the teacher **offered** to help me.

5. I _____(make) the list for the party before she **called**.

Questions are formed by using "Had + subject + been + verb + ing?"

PAST PERFECT PROGRESSIVE QUESTIONS			
Had I **been working?**		**Had** he **been working?**	
Had you **been working?**		**Had** she **been working?**	
Had we **been working?**		**Had** it **been working?**	
Had they **been working?**			

Use the verb in parentheses to make Past Perfect Progressive questions.

1. _____ Arthur _____(read) before the teacher **got** here?

2. _____she_____(wash) the dishes before I **started** helping?

3. _____ he _____(go) to the movies before **then?**

4. _____ you _____(learn) the verbs before I **taught** you?

5. How many hours _____ you _____ (walk) before we **found** you?

Negative: I hadn't been working, You, We, They hadn't been working

He hadn't been working, She hadn't been working, It hadn't been working

Use the verb in parentheses to make Past Perfect Progressive negative:

1. They _____(not/ work) when the **teacher walked** in.

2. She _____(not/ write) anything until **I told** her to.

Examples of the Present and Past tenses:

(This is an example of how Americans mix the tenses when speaking. The paragraph is color-coded to the tenses on Chart A.)

I usually wake up around 10:00 A.M. On certain occasions, I have woken up much later than that. For some reason, I woke up at 7:00 this morning. I had been dreaming something wonderful before I woke up. I had dreamed about my family and my house. I was dreaming about my dog when the alarm went off. I have been thinking about my home and my country ever since then. Now, I am trying not to feel homesick!

Simple Rules for Present and Past Tenses

1. Simple Present is used for routines, habits and schedules.

   It is also used to state facts and general truths.

   (It may also be used in the future for discussing scheduled events.)

2. Present Progressive is used for events and actions going on right now.

   (It may also be used with future, if the future time is stated.)

3. Past Simple is used for events and actions that started and finished at a specific time in the past.

4. Past Progressive is used to show an event that was in progress at a certain time in the past.

5. Present Perfect is used when there is no need to express a specific time. A present perfect event has happened at any time in the past up until the time of speaking. It doesn't necessarily continue until the present, but it is somehow relevant to the present conversation. It should never be used with a specific time.

6. Present Perfect Progressive is used to show an action that was taking place from a specific time in the past up until right now.

7. Past Perfect is used to show the relationship between two past events.

   A past perfect event takes place before another event mentioned in the simple past.

8. Past Perfect Progressive is used to express the length of time an action had been going on before another event in the simple past stopped it.

Future Tenses at a Glance

B

PRESENT

FUTURE

Specific Time in the Future

By the time she gets here
By then
By that time

X 1. I will play

X 2. I'm going to play

4. I will have played

6. If I finish

7. After I eat

3. I will be playing

5. I will have been playing

1. Future Simple

2. Future Intention

3. Future Progressive

4. Future Perfect

5. Future Perfect Progressive

6. Future Conditional

7. Future Time Clause

© 2011 Randi Mitchell Austin, Texas

Part Two: Future Tenses

Description of Chart B: Future Tenses at a Glance

a) The curved dotted lines mean "activity" or "progression"- something that is on-going for a length of time. (These are the progressive tenses.)

b) The solid curved lines mean that an action or event is completed.

c) The double vertical lines represent a specific time in the future. You can make it any time you want to use as an example: "At 2:00, we will be studying."

d) In this chart, there are 5 tenses and 2 "Future Clauses," which students also need to learn when they study the Future.

There are two constructions for future simple: "Will" and "Be going to."

For differentiation, we call "Will" the Future Simple and "Be going to" the Future Intention.

1. **FUTURE SIMPLE = Will. "Will"** is shown with a green **X,** and can take place at any time after the present. If the speaker needs to refer to a specific time with **"will,"** the time must be spoken. **"Will"** is used for spur-of-the-moment decisions and predictions.

2. **FUTURE INTENTION = Be Going to. "Be going to"** is shown with a pink **X.** It is called **Future Intention** because it usually means the speaker has a plan. This tense is used for any action that will take place at some time after the present. Specific times must be spoken. It is used for plans already made before the time of speaking.

3. **FUTURE PROGRESSIVE** is used to talk about an action that will be taking place at a specific time in the future. It is shown in a royal blue dotted line, and is dissected by a **vertical double line** that refers to a specific **event** or **time** in the future.

4. **FUTURE PERFECT** is shown in a solid lime-green line and refers to a particular action that will be completed by a specific time in the future (the vertical double line).

5. **FUTURE PERFECT PROGRESSIVE** is shown by the purple dotted line, referring to an on-going action. The line refers to an action which will have been going on for a certain amount of time by the specific time in the future (the vertical double line).

6. **FUTURE CONDITIONAL** refers to a condition clause that is often used with the future. If the condition in the **"If"** clause takes place, then the action in the main clause will also take place. **Future Conditional** clauses are always in the **Present Simple.** So this condition is shown in an orange line that leads from the simple present to the future.

7. **FUTURE TIME CLAUSE** is shown in the same way as a conditional clause, only in brown to show that there is a difference. The **Future Time Clause** begins with a time word, such as **"before," "after,"** or **"when."** A dependent time clause is always in the **Present Simple** tense when used with a future independent clause. The main clause will be in the future.

1) The Future Simple: "Cars will fly."

- **Future Simple** is shown with the **green "X"**, and can happen at any time in the future.

- **"Will"** often suggests that a speaker will do something voluntarily. (willingly) A voluntary action is one the speaker offers to do for someone else. Often, we use "will" to respond to someone else's complaint or request for help. We also use "will" when we request that someone help us or volunteer to do something for us. Similarly, we use "will not" or "won't" when we refuse to voluntarily do something.

- **"Will"** refers to a spur-of-the-moment decision which a speaker makes in response to a certain situation. **Example: "I can't hear the TV."** **Response: "I'll turn it up."**

- **"Will"** is also used for predictions. **Example: "In the future, we will have phone watches."**

The Future Simple is formed like this: Subject + will + base form verb.

Note: In all of the following charts, "you" also refers to plural.

FUTURE SIMPLE STATEMENTS: Affirmative			
I	**will go**	he	**will go**
you	**will go**	she	**will go**
we	**will go**	it	**will go**
they	**will go**		

code for "will"
and "be going to"

Some signal words for the Future Simple:

Perhaps

Someday

Okay

Yes

"The phone is ringing." "Okay, **I'll get it.**"

"**Will** you **help** me?" "Yes, **I will.**"

FUTURE SIMPLE	
PRESENT	**FUTURE**
	X 1. I will play

Practice: Future Simple

Use the verb in parentheses and change it to the Future Simple tense:

1. The stars _____ (be) visible tonight. The sky is clear.

2. He hung up on me! Don't worry. He _____ (call) you right back.

3. The phone is ringing. "I _____ get it."

4. In the future people _____ (own) robots to do their shopping.

5. I _____ (buy) one to do my housework!

Questions in Future Simple are formed with Will + subject + base form of any verb

FUTURE SIMPLE QUESTIONS		
Will I **go?**	**Will** he **go?**	
Will you **go?**	**Will** she **go?**	
Will we **go?**	**Will** it **go?**	
Will they **go?**		

Use the verb in parentheses and change it to make Future Simple questions:

1. _____ cars ever_____(fly)?

2. Yes, someday they _____ (be) electric and they_____ (fly)!

3. When _____ people _____ (start) taking care of the

   Earth?

4. _____ you _____ (help) me with these groceries?

5. _____ you _____ (turn) on the fan, please?

Negative: I will not (won't) go, You won't go, We won't go, They won't go

He won't go, She won't go, It won't go

Use the verb in parentheses and change it to the Future Simple negative:

1. She _____ (not/ go) to school today.

2. We _____ (not/ see) them tomorrow.

2) Future Intention: (Be Going to) "I'm going to play"

- Future Intention is shown in the **Pink "X"**, and can happen at any time in the future.

- The auxiliary verb **going to** is used in talking about intentions. (An intention is a plan for the future that you have already thought about.)

- The plan has been made before the time of speaking.

Future Intention is formed like this:

Subject + be + going to + base form of verb

(**Be** conjugates with the subject)

FUTURE INTENTION STATEMENTS: Affirmative		
I **am going to work**	he	**is going to work**
you **are going to work**	she	**is going to work**
we **are going to work**	it	**is going to work**
they **are going to work**		

code for "will"
and "be going to"

Signal words for Future Intention:

Next month	This afternoon
Tonight	Next semester
Tomorrow	This weekend
Next Year	Later

FUTURE INTENTION	
PRESENT	**FUTURE**
	X 1. I'm going to play

Future time clause: When, Before, After

When I finish my work, I'm going to play."

Practice: Future Intention

Use the verb in parentheses and change it to Future Intention:

1. I _____ (go) on vacation next month.

2. I _____ (visit) my aunt in Florida.

3. My brother _____ (meet) me there.

4. My family _____ (rent) a house on the ocean.

5. We _____ (stay) for two weeks!

Questions: Be + subject + going to + base form verb (Be conjugates with subject.)

FUTURE INTENTION QUESTIONS	
Am I going to work?	Is he going to work?
Are you going to work?	Is she going to work?
Are we going to work?	Is it going to work?
Are they going to work?	

Use the verb in parentheses and change it to make Future Intention questions:

1. _____ you _____ (play) soccer tomorrow?

2. _____ he _____ (go) to college?

3. When _____ they _____ (call) us?

4. What time _____ she _____ (be) here?

5. _____ I _____ (get) presents for my birthday?

Negative: 1st way - I'm not going to work, You aren't going to work, We aren't going to work, They aren't going to work
He's not going to work, She's not going to work, It's not going to work
2nd way - (I =same), You're not going to work, We're not going to work, They're not going to work.
He isn't going to work, She isn't going to work, It isn't going to work

Use the verb in parentheses and change it to make Future Intention negative:

1. He _____ (not/ play) football tonight.

2. They _____ (not/ finish) their homework before supper.

3) Future Progressive: "I will be playing"

- Future Progressive is shown with the royal blue dotted line directly under the vertical line which says: "specific time in the future"

- Future Progressive is used to put emphasis on an action that will be taking place at a specific time in the future.

- Example: "At 2:00 this afternoon, I will be leaving for the Bahamas."

Form Future Progressive as follows: Subject + will + be + verb + ing

FUTURE PROGRESSIVE STATEMENTS: Affirmative			
I	will be going	he	will be going
you	will be going	she	will be going
we	will be going	it	will be going
they	will be going		

Words that signal Future Progressive:

By that time

By then

At that time

Tomorrow

In one year

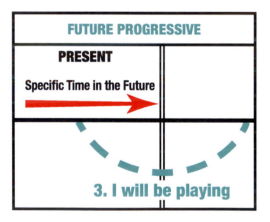

Practice: Future Progressive

Use the verb in parentheses to form the Future Progressive:

1. Don't bother calling me tonight. I _____ (study).

2. They_____(go) out to dinner tonight

3. Tomorrow at 9:00 A.M. he _____ (leave) for California.

4. If they come at midnight, I _____ (sleep.)

5. Tomorrow when she comes, I _____ (work.)

Questions are formed as follows: Will **+ subject +** be **+ verb +** ing

FUTURE PROGRESSIVE QUESTIONS			
Will I	**be working?**	**Will** he	**be working?**
Will you	**be working?**	**Will** she	**be working?**
Will we	**be working?**	**Will** it	**be working?**
Will they	**be working?**		

Use the verb in parentheses to form the Future Progressive questions:

1. _____ (you/ study) tomorrow night?

2. _____ (he/ work) this summer?

3. When _____ (they/ graduate)?

4. What time _____ (we/ go) to the store?

5. _____ (you/ go) to the post office on your way?

Negative: Use the verb in parentheses to form the Future Progressive negative:

1. He _____ (not/ do) the dishes tonight.

2. They _____ (not/ stay) outside for long. It's cold!

4) Future Perfect: "I will have played"

- **Future Perfect** is shown by the green solid line, which ends at the specific time in the future, (vertical double lines.)

- **Future Perfect** is used to express the idea that something will occur before another event or time in the future.

  Example: By 2:00 this afternoon, I will have finished these invitations.

Future Perfect is formed as follows:

Subject+ will + have + past participle

FUTURE PERFECT STATEMENTS: Affirmative			
I	will have gone	he	will have gone
you	will have gone	she	will have gone
we	will have gone	it	will have gone
they	will have gone		

Signal words for Future Perfect:

By then

By that time

By tomorrow

By next week

By 3:0

Future time clause: By the time she gets here, we will have eaten.

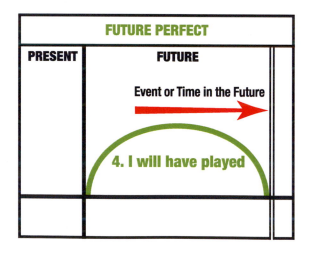

Practice: Future Perfect

Use the verb in parentheses to form the Future Perfect:

1. By 5:00 tomorrow, I _____ (finish) this job.

2. When you get here, we _____ (already / eat).

3. By the time she starts her paper, I _____ (hand) mine in.

4. If I start the dishes now, I _____ (wash) them
   all by the time you get here!

5. By next week, he_____ (graduate).

Questions are formed as follows: Will + subject + have + past participle

Use the verb in parentheses to make Future Perfect questions:

1. _____ (he/buy) the new car by the time we go on vacation?

2. _____ (we/finish) this test by 3:00?

3. _____ (she/learn) French by the time she goes to France?

4. _____ (we/complete) this report before the boss gets here?

5. _____ (you/call) her before I get there?

Negative: I won't have gone, You won't have gone, We won't have gone, They won't have gone

He won't have gone, She won't have gone, It won't have gone

Use the verb in parentheses to make Future Perfect negative:

1. We _____ (not/ see) the play by then.

2. She _____ (not/do) the report by tomorrow morning.

5) Future Perfect Progressive: "I will have been playing"

- **Future Perfect Progressive** is shown with a purple dotted line that ends at a specific time in the future, (vertical double line.)

- **Future Perfect** is used to express an action that will be going on before a certain event or time in the future. Use it to emphasize the length of time of the activity.

  Example: By tomorrow, we **will have been traveling** for two weeks.

Future Perfect Progressive is formed as follows:

Subject + **will** + **have** + **been** + **verb** + **ing**

FUTURE PERFECT PROGRESSIVE STATEMENTS: Affirmative			
I	will have been working	he	will have been working
you	will have been working	she	will have been working
we	will have been working	it	will have been working
they	will have been working		

Words that signal Future Perfect Progressive:

By that time

By then

By 3:00

By next week

Future time clause: By the time she gets here, we will have been studying **for 2 hours.**

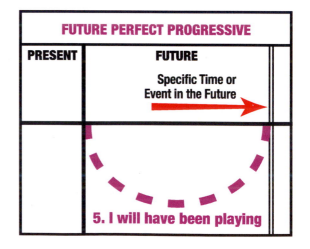

FUTURE PERFECT PROGRESSIVE

PRESENT	FUTURE
	Specific Time or Event in the Future →

5. I will have been playing

Practice: Future Perfect Progressive

Use the verb in parentheses to form the Future Perfect Progressive:

1. She _____ (work) for three hours by the time we get there.

2. When I finally finish this report, I _____ (write) for five hours straight.

3. He _____ (travel) for a week by the time he gets to Paris.

4. By this time tomorrow, she _____ (drive) for 3 days.

5. By the time we land, we _____ (fly) for 20 hours.

Questions are formed as follows: Will + subject + have + been + verb+ ing

FUTURE PERFECT PROGRESSIVE QUESTIONS			
Will I	**have been working?**	**Will** he	**have been working?**
Will you	**have been working?**	**Will** she	**have been working?**
Will we	**have been working?**	**Will** it	**have been working?**
Will they	**have been working?**		

Use the verb in parentheses to make Future Perfect Progressive questions:

1. How long _____ (we/study) by the time we finish this chapter ?

2. _____ (you/ travel) for a month by the time you get home ?

3. _____ (we/walk) for two hours by the time we get to the store ?

4. _____ (our teacher/ read) that book for an hour by the time she finishes ?

5. How long _____(they/ cooking) by then?

Negative: I will not (won't) have been working, You won't have been working, We won't have been working, They won't have been working He won't have been working, She won't have been working, It won't have been working **Use the verb in parentheses to make Future Perfect Progressive negative:**

1. We _____(not/ travel) for too long by that time.

2. He _____(not/ paint) the kitchen before we get there.

Clauses used with the future tense

Many times when we speak of future events, we use a conditional clause or a time clause. Both of these must always remain in the Present Simple.

6) Future Conditional: "If I finish, I will play."

 The Conditional Cause is shown with the orange solid line going from the "Present Tense" and leading to the "Future."

- In sentences with a condition, there is an "if" clause and a "result" clause. If the condition in the "if" clause happens, then the event in "result" clause will happen.

  Example: If it rains, we will stay home.

- The dependant clause is stated the same in a question.

  Example: If it rains, will we stay home?

- If the conditional clause is in the beginning of the sentence, use a comma.

- Don't use a comma if the conditional clause is in the middle of the sentence.

Example: If she comes, we will give her the present. We will give her the present if she comes.

FUTURE CONDITIONAL	
PRESENT	**FUTURE**
	X we will stay home.
6. If it rains	

QR code for Conditional and Time Clause

Practice: Future Conditional

1. If he _____ (come), we will tell him then.

2. If it _____ (rain), we won't go to the park.

3. If the sun _____ (shine) tomorrow, we're going to go to the beach!

4. Yes, and if the waves _____ (be) good, we're going to go surfing!

5. If she _____ (call) you, will you call me?

7) Future Time Clauses: "When I finish, I will play."

- The time clause is shown in a brown solid line going from the "present tense" and leading into the "future."

- A time clause can be used with the future. It forms a dependent clause in the simple present tense.

- Time Clauses: Before – When – After - As soon as – Once – Until

- When the time clause is in the beginning of the sentence, **use a comma.**

  Don't use a comma when the time is in the middle of the sentence.

- Examples: Before she gets here, we will set the table.

    We will set the table when she gets here.

    After she gets here, we will call the family.

    We will call the family when she gets here.

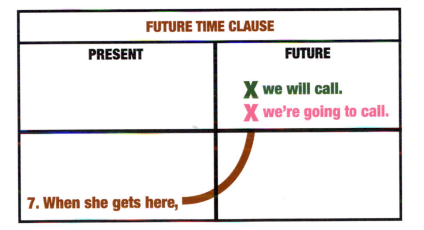

QR code for Conditional and Time Clause

Practice: Future Time Clauses

1. After you _____ (get) home, I'll be leaving for work.

2. When the plane _____ (arrive), we're going to go to baggage claim.

3. Before you _____ (paint) that wall, he's going to paint the ceiling.

4. After he _____ (study), he's going to go dancing.

5. When he _____ (finish), he'll call us.

Examples of each tense:

1. In the future, cars will fly. (Prediction)

    The phone is ringing. "I'll get it!" (Impromptu decision)

2. I'm going to go to an American university.

    (Plan or intention, already decided before the time of speaking)

3. I will be eating dinner with my friends tomorrow night.

    (Activity in progress at specific time in the future)

4. By then, I will have studied all the chapters.

    (Action will be completed by a specific time in future)

5. By then, I will have been studying for 2 hours.

    (Amount of time of an activity by a certain time in the future)

6. If it rains, we won't go. (If the condition in the dependent clause is satisfied,

    the independent clause will happen)

7. When she gets here, I'm going to give her the letter.

    (When, after, before the first activity happens, the 2nd will happen)

Simple Rules for Future Tenses:

1. "Will" is used for spur-of-the-moment decisions.

   "Will" question in Future Simple can make a request.

2. "Going to" means that the speaker already has a plan.

   In predictions, "going to" is more certain than "will."

3. "Will" question in Future Progressive asks about future plan.

   What will you be doing at a specific time in the future?

   (It is also a roundabout way of asking for a favor.)

   Example: "Will you be going by the Post Office later?" (Indirect)

   "Then will you get me a stamp?" (Direct)

4. By the time you get here, I will have studied all the chapters.

   Watch for the tense of a verb following *"By the time"*.

   If it is present, it signals a future perfect clause.

5. By then, (By the time you call,) I will have been studying for 2 hours.

   Use future perfect progressive when you want to emphasize the length of time of an activity.

6. Conditional clause is in the present; main clause is in the future.

   Conditional clause = (IF + SIMPLE PRESENT)

7. Future time clause is in the present; main clause is in the future.

   Future time clause = (When, Before, After + SIMPLE PRESENT)

   Remember:

   Present Simple can be used for the future on schedules.

   "The train leaves at 10:00 tomorrow."

   Present Progressive can be used for future, if the future time is stated.

   "I'm leaving for Houston tomorrow."

Workbook Section

Use the List of Signal Words to help you with these exercises.

It is located in the back of the book in Appendix **A5**.

The list is perforated so you can tear them out and use them in the future.

There are also perforated charts of the Verbs in Appendix **A6**.

Workbook

Part 1: Present and Past Tenses

Exercise 1: Practice the Tenses - Present and Past

Fill in the blank with the proper tense of the verb in parentheses.

1. Sara always _____ (study) at the library.

2. They _____ (play) monopoly at the moment.

3. I _____ (take) that course two years ago.

4. While I _____ (study), my brother

   _____ (watch) TV.

5. I _____ (not/ finish) my housework yet.

6. I _____ (not/travel) at all in 2010.

7. As soon as the students _____ (finish) the assignment, **the**

   teacher_____ (collect) the papers.

8. I _____ (work) on this research paper all

   week, and it's still not done!

9. Yesterday I _____ (go) to the cinema.

10. I _____ (never/hear) anything like it!

11. Right now I _____ (talk) to my cousin on the computer.

12. She often _____ (go) out to eat.

13. Why _____ (you / call) me so early? Go back to bed!

14. The last time I _____ (go) to that restaurant, the food_____ (be) bad.

15. We _____ (work) on that test for 3 hours

    when the teacher _____(tell) us that time was up.

Exercise 2: Mixing the tenses

Fill in the blank with the proper tense of the word in parentheses. Use the signal words and colors to help you. (The signal words are in the color of the tense you need.)

1. I **usually** _____ (wake) up at 5:30 to walk the dog.

2. **Lately,** I _____ (take) my neighbor's dog for a walk, also.

3. I _____ (teach) English **for forty years**, and I am still teaching.

4. **Last year,** I _____ (live) in Peru.

5. **Normally,** the people there _____ (speak) Spanish.

6. **While** I _____ (live) there, I _____ (teach) English to the Spanish people.

7. **One day,** I _____ (take) a trip to the mountains.

8. **That day,** I _____(see) the ruins of a city that the Incas_____ (build) **500 years before.**

9. Now I am back in Texas, and the weather is much warmer. But it **frequently** _____ (rain).

10. I wonder when it will stop raining. It _____ (rain) **for days.**

11. I couldn't go to the party **last night.** I _____(study).

12. Carolyn has been working on her paper for two days. ***By the time** I **started** mine, she _____(finish) hers.

13. ***By the time** we **got** to Italy we _____ (travel) for 3 days.

14 **Last night** my friend _____ (Invite) me to a movie.

15. I **told** her that I _____(already/see) the movie, so I _____ (not/want) to go again.

*When you see "By the time", look at the tense of the verb following it to decide if you need future perfect or past perfect.

Exercise 3: Question Forms

Answer these questions for practice.

1. **What is something you do every day?**

   _____

2. **Have you ever been to Paris?**

   _____

3. **What did you do last night?**

   _____

4. **What had you done before you came to school today?**

   _____

5. **What are you doing right now?**

   _____

6. **What have you been doing since you came to the U.S.?**

   _____

7. **What were you doing when the bell rang?**

   _____

8. **What had you been studying before you started studying English?**

   _____

Exercise 4:

Fill in the blank with the proper tense of the verb in parentheses.

1. I_____ (read) the newspaper every day.
2. _____ you ever _____ (go) to Japan?
3. He said he _____ never _____ (kiss) a girl before that night.
4. Dan _____ (buy) a new car last month.
5. She _____ (meet) her boss before she even _____ (go) to work there.
6. It's been a long time since we _____ (see) her.
7. I _____ (not / hear) from Susan for two weeks now.
8. A: Where is Jimmy?

   B: He's outside.

   A: What _____ he_____? (do)

   B: He _____ (clean) the garage.

9. Look! It _____! (snow)
10. _____ you _____ (read) any good books lately?
11. Tom _____ (not/be) at school yesterday.
12. They _____ (drink) alcohol before last night.
13. It looks like Sarah _____ (go) to the gym lately.
14. Joan and Sam _____ (play) cards all day!
15. They _____ (live) there since they were children.
16. It usually _____ (rain) a lot in April.
17. Stop talking! I_____ (study) my lessons.
18. She _____ (not / call) me last night.
19. Paul _____ (not / work) at the moment.
20. _____ Susan _____ (live) in California? Yes, she does.
21. This is the best book I _____ (ever / read).
22. How long _____ she _____ (be) in Paris before her boyfriend came?
23. Who _____ (call) you yesterday while you _____ (study)?
24. Who _____ you _____ (see) at the library yesterday?
25. Susan and John _____ (know) each other for over 25 years.
26. I _____ (already / finish) my homework.
27. How long _____ she _____ (work) there when you met her?
28. How long _____ she _____ (be) in Chicago?
29. I _____ (meet) her a couple of days ago.
30. He is the most stupid man I _____ (ever / meet).
31. How long ago _____ they_____ (leave)?

Exercise 5: Multiple Choice - Present and Past

Choose the best answer to complete the sentence:

1. _____ the firefighters were putting out the flames, the paramedics were helping the injured.

    a. While   c. Next

    b. During   d. After

2. Jack cut himself while he _____.

    a. shaving   c. was shaving

    b. shaves   d. is shaving

3. _____ been to that restaurant before we went last night?

    a. Had you   c. You had

    b. Have you   d. You have

4. Jennifer never _____ in the ocean.

    a. is swimming   c. swimming

    b. swim   d. swims

5. The story is about an actress who has won the award _____.

    a. yesterday   c. a few weeks ago

    b. last year   d. three times

6. The journalists _____ on the war since March.

    a. reported   c. has reported

    b. had reported   d. have reported

7. My mother has taught English _____ twenty years.

    a. in   c. during

    b. for   d. since

(cont'd on next page)

8. What _____ doing right now?

    a. you are   c. you were

    b. are you   d. have you

9. We _____several speeches in the past few days.

    a. had given   c. have given

    b. are giving   d. will give

10. Where _____ you go to school?

    a. have   c. had

    b. did   d. was

11. When the bell rang yesterday, we _____ a composition in class.

    a. wrote   c. write

    b. were writing   d. writing

12. Larry went to New York City last year because he _____ to visit there for a long time.

    a. has wanted   c. had been wanted

    b had wanted   d. is wanted

13. When I came home, the house smelled so good, because my mom _____dinner.

    a. was cook   c. did cook

    b. had been cooking   d. cooking

14. The children _____ when their father came home.

    a. slept   c. were sleeping

    b. are sleeping   d. sleep

15. I like to see movies. I_____ to the movies since I was a child.

    a. have been going   c. have been

    b. had been going   d. have goes

Exercise 6: Try writing a paragraph with all the past tenses.

Many times, when we are speaking to people, we tell them about an event in our past. Now you can use all these tenses to tell stories about yourself!

Use the following as an example:

I lived in California 20 years ago. I went to college there. But before I went to college, I had been a professional skier. I had been trying to get into the Olympics before I had a serious accident. While I was skiing at Lake Tahoe, I hit a rock and flipped up into the air. I landed on my head and sprained my neck. Ever since then I have been a student. I have been studying how to teach ESL. Now I am happy to be a teacher. I am enjoying meeting students from all over the world!

Now you try!

_____

_____

_____

_____

_____

_____

_____

_____

_____

Part 2: Future Tenses

Exercise 1: Practice the Tenses: Future

Fill in the blank with the proper tense of the verb in parentheses.

1. The stars _____ (not/ be) visible tonight. It's too cloudy.

2. I _____ (visit) my aunt in Florida next month.

3. Don't bother calling me tonight. I_____ (study.)

4. By 5:00 tomorrow, I _____ (finish) this job.

5. He _____ (travel) for a week by the time he gets to Paris.

6. If he _____ (come), we will tell him then.

7. If the plane _____ (arrive) on time, we're going to go to the movies.

8. When he _____ (finish), he'll call us.

9. The phone is ringing. "I'_____ get it."

10. What _____ (do) on your vacation?

11. At this time tomorrow, he _____ (leave) for California.

12. He hung up on me! Don't worry. He _____ (call) you right back.

13. My brother _____ (meet) me at the mall in an hour.

14. By next week, he_____ (graduate.)

15. By the time we land, we _____ (fly) for 20 hours.

Exercise 2: Question Forms

Answer these questions for practice.

1. These packages are heavy. **Will you get the door for me?**

   _____

2. **Are you going to go to Paris on your vacation?**

   _____

3. **Will you be practicing the piano this afternoon?**

   _____

4. **Will you have practiced for two hours by 5:00?**

   _____

5. **Will you have been practicing for more than four hours by dinner time?**

   _____

6. **If it rains, will we still go to the park?**

   _____

7. **When she comes, are you going to tell her about the party?**

   _____

Exercise 3

Choose between "Will" or "Be Going To." Use contractions where possible.

Remember: "Will" is a spur-of-the-moment decision. "Be going to" is a plan already made before the time of speaking.

1. It's so hot in here. OK, I _____ (turn) on the air conditioner.

2. Why is the oven on? I _____ (bake) some cookies.

3. In the fall I _____ (go) to medical school.

4. After we eat lunch, we _____ (take) a walk on the beach.

5. The phone is ringing! I _____ (get) it!

6. These packages are heavy. Here, I _____ (open) the door for you.

7. What _____ (he/do) on vacation?

8. I'm so sleepy that I can't study. I _____ (make) you a cup of coffee.

9. May I borrow a pen? I _____ (write) a letter.

10. That television is so loud! OK, I _____ (turn) it down.

Exercise 4: Predictions:

Choose between "going to" and "will" (Be going to" is a stronger prediction than "Will")

1. The Bears are the best team this year. I know they _____ (win) the

   championship.

2. I think that man _____ (run) for president next year.

3. In the future, people probably _____ (have) flying cars.

4. Look at how black the sky is! It _____ (rain).

Exercise 5:

Choose the best answer (A, B, C) to complete the sentence.

1. If people _____ things, there will be more problems in the future.
   A. don't recycle
   B. aren't recycle
   C. aren't recycle/are going be

2. If Peter _____ to the movie with us, his girlfriend will be angry.
   A. will go
   B. goes
   C. going to

3. He'll feel better if he _____.
   A. is going to exercise
   B. will exercise
   C. exercises

4. Maggie and Sam are _____ married next week.
   A. going to get
   B. get
   C. won't getting

5. The teacher _____ the test before she knows our final grades.
   A. is check
   B. are checking
   C. will check

6. Who is _____ with us to the beach on Sunday?
   A. comes
   B. going to come
   C. will coming

7. As soon as John _____ his girlfriend, he will kiss her.
   A. will see
   B. sees
   C. is seeing

(cont'd. on next page)

8. By the time we get to Moscow, we _____ for two weeks.
   A. will travel
   B. are going to travel
   C. will have been traveling

9. When we get there he _____ all the furniture.
   A. will be moved
   B. will have moved
   C. will be move

10. After Becky _____ the picture, she'll take a break.
   A. will hang
   B. is going to hang
   C. hangs

11. Choose the correct question:
   A. What do you doing?
   B. What you are going to do?
   C. What are you going to do?

12. The bus _____ at 8:00.
   A. comes
   B. does come
   C. has coming

13. By the time I finish my dinner, the sun _____.
   A. won't set
   B. sets
   C. will have set

14. Person A: The phone is ringing and my hands are full.
    Could someone please answer it?
       Person B: I _____ it.
   A. answer
   B. will answer
   C. am going to answer

15. After you call the doctor's office, you _____ when the doctor is available.
   A. will found out
   B. will find out
   C. going to find out

Exercise 6:
Now write a paragraph using the Future tenses.

We use the future in conversation to tell others about our plans and hopes for the future.

Use the following as an example:

I think that people will use the internet a lot more in the future. I think I am going to make this an E-book. That means I will be writing a lot more in the next few months. By next year I will have made an E- book. I will have been working on it for 3 years by then. If I find that it is helping students, I will be very happy. When you are finished with this book, will you understand the tenses better? I hope you have a great future in your career, now that you speak English!

Now you try!

_____

_____

_____

_____

_____

_____

_____

Answer Key:

Past and Present Tenses

Exercise 1: Past and Present Tenses

1. studies
2. 're playing
3. took
4. was studying/ was watching
5. have not finished
6. didn't travel
7. had finished/ collected
8. have been working
9. went
10. have never heard
11. am talking
12. goes
13. are you calling
14. went/ was
15. had been working/ told

Exercise 2: Mixing the Tenses (use signal words)

1. wake
2. have been taking
3. have been teaching
4. lived
5. speak
6. was living/ was teaching
7. took
8. saw/ had built
9. rains
10. has been raining
11. was studying
12. will have finished
13. had been traveling
14. invited
15. had already seen / did not want

Exercise 3: Question Forms

1. I study every day. (Simple Present)
2. I have never been to Paris. (Present Perfect)
3. Last night I went to a movie. (Simple Past)
4. I had showered before I came to school today. (Past Perfect)
5. I am studying right now. (Present Progressive)
6. Since I came to the U.S. I have been speaking English. (Present Perfect Progressive)
7. I was talking to my friend when the bell rang. (Past Progressive)
8. Before I started studying English, I had been studying engineering. (Past Perfect Progressive)

Exercise 4: Fill in the blank

1. read
2. Have / gone
3. had/ kissed
4. bought
5. had met/went
6. have seen
7. have not heard
8. is/ doing? / 's cleaning
9. 's snowing
10. Have/ read
11. wasn't
12. had drunk
13. has been going
14. have been playing
15. have lived/ have been living
16. rains
17. 'm studying
18. didn't call
19. isn't working
20. Does/ live
21. Have/ read
22. had/ been
23. called/ were studying
24. did/ see
25. have known
26. have already finished
27. had/ been working
28. has/ been
29. met
30. have ever met
31. did / leave

Exercise 5: Multiple Choice

1. a
2. c
3. a
4. d
5. d
6. d
7. b
8. b
9. c
10. b
11. b
12. b
13. b
14. c
15. a

Exercise 6: Answers will vary

Part 2

Practice Exercises: Future

Exercise 1: Practice the Future Tenses

1. won't
2. 'm going to
3. will be studying
4. will have finished
5. will have been traveling
6. comes
7. arrives
8. finishes
9. 'll
10. are you going to do
11. will be leaving
12. 'll call
13. is going to meet
14. will have graduated
15. will have been flying

Exercise 2: Questions

1. Yes, I'll help you. (Future Simple)

2. No, I'm not going to go to Paris on my vacation. (Future Intention)

3. Yes, I will be practicing the piano this afternoon. (Future Progressive)

4. Yes, I will have practiced for 2 hours by 5:00. (Future Perfect)

5. Yes, I will have been practicing for more than four hours by dinner time. (Future Perfect Progressive)

6. If it rains, we won't go to the park. (Conditional Future)

7. When she comes, I will tell her about the party. (Future Time Clause)

Exercise 3: "Will" or "Going to"

1. 'll
2. 'm going to
3. 'm going to go
4. 're going to take
5. 'll get
6. 'll open
7. is he going to do
8. 'll make
9. 'm going to write
10. 'll turn

Exercise 4: Predictions

1. 're going to win
2. will
3. will
4. 's going to

Exercise 5: Choose the Best Answer

1. A
2. B
3. C
4. A
5. C
6. B
7. B
8. C
9. B
10. C
11. C
12. A
13. C
14. B
15. B

Exercise 6: Answers will vary

Appendices

A1: Spelling Rules for Present Simple Third Person Singular in Affirmative Form

1) Add the letter **"s"** to the *base form* of the verb in present simple affirmative sentences for the third person singular.

   He talks.　　　　**She helps.**　　　　**It works.**

2) If the base form of the verb ends in **"-sh"**, **"-ch"**, **"-ss"**, letter **"x"**, letter **"z"** and vowel **"o"**, we add **"-es".***

   He teaches Spanish.　　　　**She washes her clothes.**

3) if the base form ends in *consonant + letter "y"*, we change "y" for letter "i" and then, we add **"es".***

   study　　　　**studies.**

   *Watch out! We <u>don't</u> add **"es"** if the verb ends in *vowel + letter "y"*. In those cases, we just add an **"s"**.

   play　　　　**plays.**

4) ***Have, do, and go*** have irregular forms for the third person Singular.

I have a car.	**He has a car.**
I do laundry.	**She does laundry.**
I go slowly.	**It goes slowly**

A2:   **Spelling rules for progressive endings** – Present, Past, Future

1) Most verbs, *add* –ing

He is talking.

2) CVC Rule:

(A) If a one-syllable word ends in a <u>consonant + vowel +consonant</u> (CVC), *double the final*

consonant and add ing.

sit = sitting   put = putting   hug = hugging

(except with **x, w, y).**

fixing, plowing, obeying

(B) In a word with more than one syllable: if the syllable with **consonant/ vowel/ consonant**

is stressed, ***double the consonant:***

prefer   preferring

(C) In a word with more than one syllable: if the syllable with **consonant/ vowel/ consonant**

<u>is not</u> stressed, ***do not double the consonant:***

benefit   benefiting

3) One -e at the end of the word

Leave out the -e.   Write – he **is** writing   Take – he **is** taking

BUT: double –e: add -ing

See   seeing

4) Verbs ending in -ie

Change 'ie' to 'y'.

lie - he **is** lying

5) Verbs ending in –c: *Change 'c' to 'ck'*   picnic - he **is** picnicking

A3:   **Spelling Rules for regular past tense verbs**

1) Add **ed** to the base form of most regular verbs.

       rain   rained

2) If the verb ends in an "e" – add only **d.**

       arrive   arrived

       like   liked

3) **CVC Rule**

    (A) *If a one-syllable verb ends in a* **consonant+ vowel + consonant (CVC), double the final**

      consonant and add **ed.**

           hug   hugged

           rub   rubbed

           (except with **w, x, and y)**

           bow   bowed

           mix   mixed

    (B) If the verb has two syllables and the final syllable is stressed, **double the consonant** and

      add **ed.**

           prefer   preferred

           omit   omitted

    (C) If the verb has two syllables and the final syllable is not stressed, **do not double the**

      consonant.

           travel   traveled

           listen   listened

4) Verbs that end in "y"

    (A) If the verb ends in **consonant + y**, change the **y** to **i** and add **ed.**

      study / studied   worry/ worried

    (B) If the verb ends in **vowel + y,** simply add **ed.**

      play / played   enjoy / enjoyed

A4: Common English Irregular Verb List – at a Glance

Base Form	Past Simple	Past Participle	3rd Person Singular	Present Participle
Abide	Abode/Abided	Abode/Abided	Abides	Abiding
Arise	Arose	Arisen	Arises	Arising
Awake	Awoke	Awoken	Awakes	Awaking
Be	Was/Were	Been	Is	Being
Bear	Bore	Born/Borne	Bears	Bearing
Beat	Beat	Beaten	Beats	Beating
Become	Became	Become	Becomes	Becoming
Begin	Began	Begun	Begins	Beginning
Behold	Beheld	Beheld	Beholds	Beholding
Bend	Bent	Bent	Bends	Bending
Bet	Bet	Bet	Bets	Betting
Bid	Bade	Bidden	Bids	Bidding
Bid	Bid	Bid	Bids	Bidding
Bind	Bound	Bound	Binds	Binding
Bite	Bit	Bitten	Bites	Biting
Bleed	Bled	Bled	Bleeds	Bleeding
Blow	Blew	Blown	Blows	Blowing
Break	Broke	Broken	Breaks	Breaking
Breed	Bred	Bred	Breeds	Breeding
Bring	Brought	Brought	Brings	Bringing
Build	Built	Built	Builds	Building
Burn	Burnt/Burned	Burnt/Burned	Burns	Burning
Burst	Burst	Burst	Bursts	Bursting
Bust	Bust	Bust	Busts	Busting
Buy	Bought	Bought	Buys	Buying
Cast	Cast	Cast	Casts	Casting
Catch	Caught	Caught	Catches	Catching
Choose	Chose	Chosen	Chooses	Choosing
Clap	Clapped	Clapped	Claps	Clapping
Cling	Clung	Clung	Clings	Clinging
Clothe	Clad/Clothed	Clad/Clothed	Clothes	Clothing
Come	Came	Come	Comes	Coming
Cost	Cost	Cost	Costs	Costing
Creep	Crept	Crept	Creeps	Creeping
Cut	Cut	Cut	Cuts	Cutting
Dare	Dared/Durst	Dared	Dares	Daring
Deal	Dealt	Dealt	Deals	Dealing
Dig	Dug	Dug	Digs	Digging
Dive	Dived/Dove	Dived	Dives	Diving
Do	Did	Done	Does	Doing
Draw	Drew	Drawn	Draws	Drawing
Dream	Dreamt/Dreamed	Dreamt/Dreamed	Dreams	Dreaming
Drink	Drank	Drunk	Drinks	Drinking

English Verb Tenses at a Glance

Base Form	Past Simple	Past Participle	3rd Person Singular	Present Participle
Drive	Drove	Driven	Drives	Driving
Dwell	Dwelt	Dwelt	Dwells	Dwelling
Eat	Ate	Eaten	Eats	Eating
Fall	Fell	Fallen	Falls	Falling
Feed	Fed	Fed	Feeds	Feeding
Feel	Felt	Felt	Feels	Feeling
Fight	Fought	Fought	Fights	Fighting
Find	Found	Found	Finds	Finding
Fit	Fit/Fitted	Fit/Fitted	Fits	Fitting
Flee	Fled	Fled	Flees	Fleeing
Fling	Flung	Flung	Flings	Flinging
Fly	Flew	Flown	Flies	Flying
Forbid	Forbade/Forbad	Forbidden	Forbids	Forbidding
Forecast	Forecast/Forecasted	Forecast/Forecasted	Forecasts	Forecasting
Foresee	Foresaw	Foreseen	Foresees	Foreseeing
Foretell	Foretold	Foretold	Foretells	Foretelling
Forget	Forgot	Forgotten	Forgets	Forgetting
Forgive	Forgave	Forgiven	Forgives	Forgiving
Forsake	Forsook	Forsaken	Forsakes	Forsaking
Freeze	Froze	Frozen	Freezes	Freezing
Frostbite	Frostbit	Frostbitten	Frostbites	Frostbiting
Get	Got	Got/Gotten	Gets	Getting
Give	Gave	Given	Gives	Giving
Go	Went	Gone/Been	Goes	Going
Grind	Ground	Ground	Grinds	Grinding
Grow	Grew	Grown	Grows	Growing
Handwrite	Handwrote	Handwritten	Handwrites	Handwriting
Hang	Hung/Hanged	Hung/Hanged	Hangs	Hanging
Have	Had	Had	Has	Having
Hear	Heard	Heard	Hears	Hearing
Hide	Hid	Hidden	Hides	Hiding
Hit	Hit	Hit	Hits	Hitting
Hold	Held	Held	Holds	Holding
Hurt	Hurt	Hurt	Hurts	Hurting
Inlay	Inlaid	Inlaid	Inlays	Inlaying
Input	Input/Inputted	Input/Inputted	Inputs	Inputting
Interlay	Interlaid	Interlaid	Interlays	Interlaying
Keep	Kept	Kept	Keeps	Keeping
Kneel	Knelt/Kneeled	Knelt/Kneeled	Kneels	Kneeling
Knit	Knit/Knitted	Knit/Knitted	Knits	Knitting
Know	Knew	Known	Knows	Knowing
Lay	Laid	Laid	Lays	laying
Lead	Led	Led	Leads	Leading
Lean	Leant/Leaned	Leant/Leaned	Leans	Leaning

English Verb Tenses at a Glance

Base Form	Past Simple	Past Participle	3rd Person Singular	Present Participle
Leave	Left	Left	Leaves	Leaving
Lend	Lent	Lent	Lends	Lending
Let	Let	Let	Lets	Letting
Lie	Lay	Lain	Lies	Lying
Light	Lit	Lit	Lights	Lighting
Lose	Lost	Lost	Loses	Losing
Make	Made	Made	Makes	Making
Mean	Meant	Meant	Means	Meaning
Meet	Met	Met	Meets	Meeting
Melt	Melted	Molten/Melted	Melts	Melting
Mislead	Misled	Misled	Misleads	Misleading
Mistake	Mistook	Mistaken	Mistakes	Mistaking
Misunderstand	Misunderstood	Misunderstood	Misunderstands	Misunderstanding
Mow	Mowed	Mown	Mows	Mowing
Overdraw	Overdrew	Overdrawn	Overdraws	Overdrawing
Overhear	Overheard	Overheard	Overhears	Overhearing
Overtake	Overtook	Overtaken	Overtakes	Overtaking
Pay	Paid	Paid	Pays	Paying
Preset	Preset	Preset	Presets	Presetting
Prove	Proved	Proven/Proved	Proves	Proving
Put	Put	Put	Puts	Putting
Quit	Quit	Quit	Quits	Quitting
Read	Read	Read	Reads	Reading
Rid	Rid/Ridded	Rid/Ridded	Rids	Ridding
Ride	Rode	Ridden	Rides	Riding
Ring	Rang	Rung	Rings	Ringing
Rise	Rose	Risen	Rises	Rising
Run	Ran	Run	Runs	Running
Saw	Sawed	Sawn/Sawed	Saws	Sawing
Say	Said	Said	Says	Saying
See	Saw	Seen	Sees	Seeing
Seek	Sought	Sought	Seeks	Seeking
Sell	Sold	Sold	Sells	Selling
Send	Sent	Sent	Sends	Sending
Set	Set	Set	Sets	Setting
Sew	Sewed	Sewn/Sewed	Sews	Sewing
Shake	Shook	Shaken	Shakes	Shaking
Shear	Shore/Sheared	Shorn/Sheared	Shears	Shearing
Shed	Shed	Shed	Sheds	Shedding
Shine	Shone	Shone	Shines	Shining
Shoe	Shod	Shod	Shoes	Shoeing
Shoot	Shot	Shot	Shoots	Shooting
Show	Showed	Shown	Shows	Showing
Shrink	Shrank	Shrunk	Shrinks	Shrinking

English Verb Tenses at a Glance

Base Form	Past Simple	Past Participle	3rd Person Singular	Present Participle
Shut	Shut	Shut	Shuts	Shutting
Sing	Sang	Sung	Sings	Singing
Sink	Sank	Sunk	Sinks	Sinking
Sit	Sat	Sat	Sits	Sitting
Slay	Slew	Slain	Slays	Slaying
Sleep	Slept	Slept	Sleeps	Sleeping
Slide	Slid	Slid	Slides	Sliding
Sling	Slung	Slung	Slings	Slinging
Slink	Slunk	Slunk	Slinks	Slinking
Slit	Slit	Slit	Slits	Slitting
Smell	Smelt/Smelled	Smelt/Smelled	Smells	Smelling
Sneak	Sneaked/Snuck	Sneaked/Snuck	Sneaks	Sneaking
Sow	Sowed	Sown	Sows	Sowing
Speak	Spoke	Spoken	Speaks	Speaking
Speed	Sped/Speeded	Sped/Speeded	Speeds	Speeding
Spell	Spelled	Spelled	Spells	Spelling
Spend	Spent	Spent	Spends	Spending
Spin	Spun	Spun	Spins	Spinning
Spit	Spat/Spit	Spat/Spit	Spits	Spitting
Split	Split	Split	Splits	Splitting
Spoil	Spoilt/Spoiled	Spoilt/Spoiled	Spoils	Spoiling
Spread	Spread	Spread	Spreads	Spreading
Spring	Sprang	Sprung	Springs	Springing
Stand	Stood	Stood	Stands	Standing
Steal	Stole	Stolen	Steals	Stealing
Stick	Stuck	Stuck	Sticks	Sticking
Sting	Stung	Stung	Stings	Stinging
Stink	Stank	Stunk	Stinks	Stinking
Stride	Strode	Stridden	Strides	Striding
Strike	Struck	Struck/Stricken	Strikes	Striking
String	Strung	Strung	Strings	Stringing
Strip	Stripped	Stripped	Strips	Stripping
Strive	Strove	Striven	Strives	Striving
Sublet	Sublet	Sublet	Sublets	Subletting
Swear	Swore	Sworn	Swears	Swearing
Sweep	Swept	Swept	Sweeps	Sweeping
Swell	Swelled	Swollen	Swells	Swelling
Swim	Swam	Swum	Swims	Swimming
Swing	Swung	Swung	Swings	Swinging
Take	Took	Taken	Takes	Taking
Teach	Taught	Taught	Teaches	Teaching
Tear	Tore	Torn	Tears	Tearing
Tell	Told	Told	Tells	Telling
Think	Thought	Thought	Thinks	Thinking

Base Form	Past Simple	Past Participle	3rd Person Singular	Present Participle
Thrive	Throve/Thrived	Thriven/Thrived	Thrives	Thriving
Throw	Threw	Thrown	Throws	Throwing
Thrust	Thrust	Thrust	Thrusts	Thrusting
Tread	Trod	Trodden	Treads	Treading
Undergo	Underwent	Undergone	Undergoes	Undergoing
Understand	Understood	Understood	Understands	Understanding
Undertake	Undertook	Undertaken	Undertakes	Undertaking
Upset	Upset	Upset	Upsets	Upsetting
Vex	Vexed	Vexed	Vexes	Vexing
Wake	Woke	Woken	Wakes	Waking
Wear	Wore	Worn	Wears	Wearing
Weave	Wove	Woven	Weaves	Weaving
Wed	Wed/Wedded	Wed/Wedded	Weds	Wedding
Weep	Wept	Wept	Weeps	Weeping
Wet	Wet	Wet	Wets	Wetting
Win	Won	Won	Wins	Winning
Wind	Wound	Wound	Winds	Winding
Withdraw	Withdrew	Withdrawn	Withdraws	Withdrawing
Withhold	Withheld	Withheld	Withholds	Withholding
Withstand	Withstood	Withstood	Withstands	Withstanding
Wring	Wrung	Wrung	Wrings	Wringing
Write	Wrote	Written	Writes	Writing

A5: **Signal Words: Present and Past Tenses**

<u>**Present Simple**</u>

Every day   Typically

In general   Generally

All the time   Normally

(Adverbs of Frequency)

Never   Rarely   Seldom   Sometimes   Frequently   Usually   Always

"I always study at the library."

<u>**Present Progressive**</u>

Right now

Right this minute

Currently

At the moment

"We're playing cards at the moment."

<u>**Past Simple:**</u>

Yesterday   After

When   Before

Last week   A month ago

In 2008   That day

The last time   One time

Specific time: "Yesterday I went to the zoo."

<u>**Past progressive**</u>

When - "I was walking down the street when I ran into my English teacher."

As long as   **While**   **Meanwhile**   **In the meantime**

Present Perfect:

Yet	Ever
Never	So far
Already	Up to now
Just	Recently
Lately	

Since/ For   Since 2008 (Specific date)   For 3 years (Amount of time)

3 times   (Do NOT use number of times with progressive)

No specific time: "I have never been to Spain."

Present perfect progressive

all day	the whole week
Recently	Lately
since 1993	for 4 years

"I have been working all day!"

Past Perfect

Never

For

Before

When

By the time – By the time I got there, she had left.

After - "After I had eaten, I took a shower."

Past Perfect Progressive

Never	When	
For	After	By 2:00
Before	By the time	By then

(some event or time in the past ended the progression) "By 2:00 I had been working on this project for 3 hours." "When she got here, I had already left."

A6:   Signal Words: Future Tenses

Future Simple

Perhaps

Someday

Okay

"Yes, I will."

Future Intention

Next month

Tonight

Next week

Tomorrow

Future Progressive

By then

At that time

Tomorrow

In one year

Future Perfect

By then

By that time

By tomorrow

By next week

By 3:00

Future Perfect Progressive

By that time

By then

By 3:00

By next week

Conditional Future

If

Future Time Clauses

Before

When

After

As soon as

Until

Once

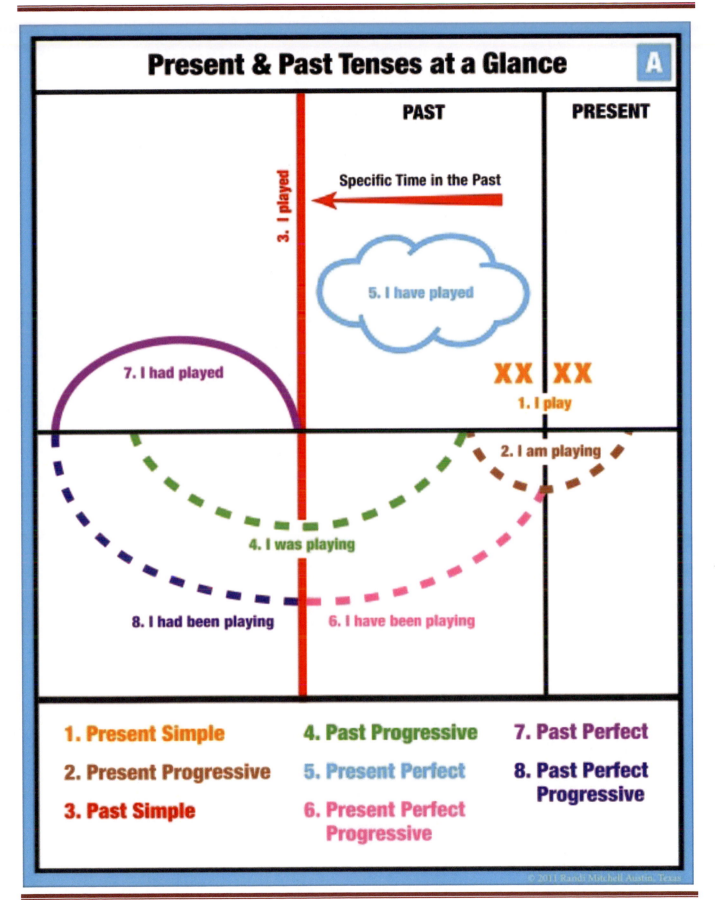

Present & Past Tenses at a Glance A

PAST   PRESENT

3. I played

Specific Time in the Past

5. I have played

7. I had played

XX XX

1. I play

2. I am playing

4. I was playing

8. I had been playing   6. I have been playing

1. Present Simple   4. Past Progressive   7. Past Perfect

2. Present Progressive   5. Present Perfect   8. Past Perfect
                                                       Progressive
3. Past Simple   6. Present Perfect
                            Progressive

© 2011 Randi Mitchell Austin, Texas

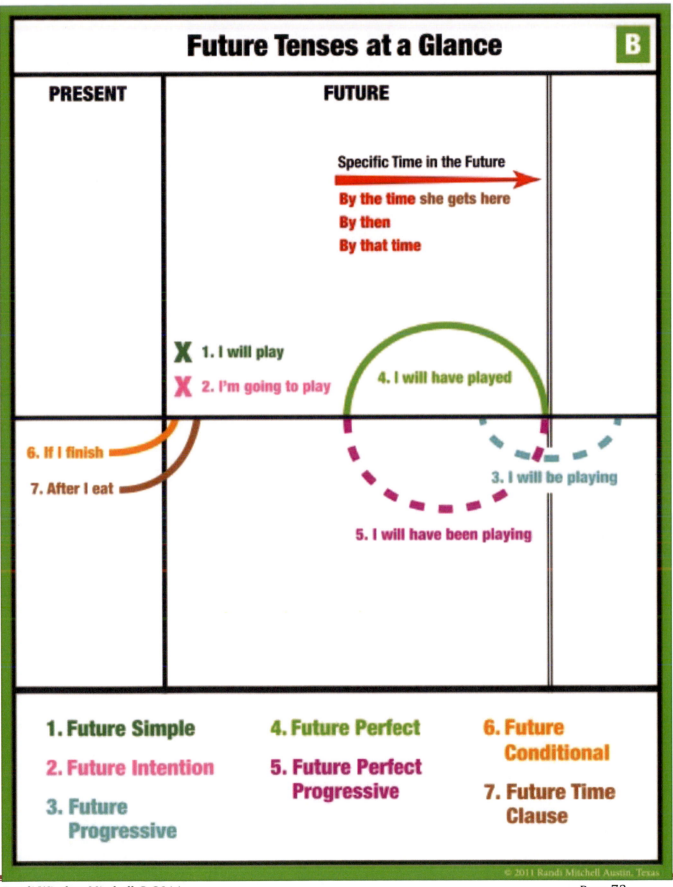

Future Tenses at a Glance   **B**

PRESENT

FUTURE

Specific Time in the Future →

By the time she gets here
By then
By that time

X 1. I will play
X 2. I'm going to play

4. I will have played

6. If I finish
7. After I eat

3. I will be playing

5. I will have been playing

1. **Future Simple**

2. **Future Intention**

3. **Future Progressive**

4. **Future Perfect**

5. **Future Perfect Progressive**

6. **Future Conditional**

7. **Future Time Clause**

English Verb Tenses at a Glance

SIMPLE		PAST	PRESENT	FUTURE
Singular	I	learned	learn	will learn
	You	learned	learn	will learn
	He/She/It	learned	learns	will learn
Plural	We	learned	learn	will learn
	You	learned	learn	will learn
	They	learned	learn	will learn
PROGRESSIVE		**PAST**	**PRESENT**	**FUTURE**
Singular	I	was learning	am learning	will be learning
	You	were learning	are learning	will be learning
	He/She/It	was learning	is learning	will be learning
Plural	We	were learning	are learning	will be learning
	You	were learning	are learning	will be learning
	They	were learning	are learning	will be learning
PERFECT		**PAST**	**PRESENT**	**FUTURE**
Singular	I	had learned	have learned	will have learned
	You	had learned	have learned	will have learned
	He/She/It	had learned	has learned	will have learned
Plural	We	had learned	have learned	will have learned
	You	had learned	have learned	will have learned
	They	had learned	have learned	will have learned
PERFECT PROGRESSIVE		**PAST**	**PRESENT**	**FUTURE**
Singular	I	had been learning	have been learning	will have been learning
	You	had been learning	have been learning	will have been learning
	He/She/It	had been learning	has been learning	will have been learning
Plural	We	had been learning	have been learning	will have been learning
	You	had been learning	have been learning	will have been learning
	They	had been learning	have been learning	will have been learning

22171215R00049